ALL ALONE

Kevin Henkes

Greenwillow Books

New York

Copyright © 1981 by Kevin Henkes. All rights reserved. No part of this book may
be reproduced or utilized in any form or by any means, electronic or mechanical,
including photocopying, recording or by any information storage and retrieval
system, without permission in writing from the Publisher, Greenwillow Books,
a division of William Morrow & Company, Inc.,
105 Madison Avenue, New York, N.Y. 10016.

Printed in the United States of America   First Edition

10 9 8 7 6 5 4 3 2 1

Library of Congress
Cataloging in Publication Data
Henkes, Kevin.   All alone.
Summary: The narrator explains why
it is sometimes nice to be alone.
[1. Solitude—Fiction] I. Title.
PZ7.H389Al   [E]   81-105
ISBN 0-688-00604-3   AACR2
ISBN 0-688-00605-1 (lib. bdg.)

To Mom, for knowing
I should take the chance

Sometimes I like to live alone, all by myself.

When I'm alone, I hear more and see more.

I hear the trees breathe in the wind.

I can see through the ground.
The roots make tangled shapes.

I feel the sun's heat all over me.

When I'm alone, I can change my size any way I like. I can be tall enough to taste the sky.

And small enough to hide behind a stone.

When it's just me, I ask myself questions
I can't answer.

I think of favorite things I've done.

Then I'm back all alone again.

When I'm alone, I look at myself inside and out.
No one looks just like me or thinks just like I do.

I wonder what my friends are doing.

Sometimes I like to live alone,
all by myself,
for just a while.